Christmas and Hanukkah Origami

by Ruth Owen

PowerKiDS
press.

New York

Published in 2013 by The Rosen Publishing Group, Inc.
29 East 21st Street, New York, NY 10010

Produced for Rosen by Ruby Tuesday Books Ltd
Editor for Ruby Tuesday Books Ltd: Mark J. Sachner
US Editor: Sara Antill
Designer: Emma Randall

Photo Credits:
Cover, 1, 3, 5, 7 (top), 7 (bottom left), 8 (bottom left), 9 (top right), 11 (bottom), 12, 17 (top right), 20, 24 (bottom left), 29 (top right) © Shutterstock; 7 (bottom right) © Elfer, Creative Commons Wikipedia.
Origami models © Ruby Tuesday Books Ltd.

Library of Congress Cataloging-in-Publication Data

Owen, Ruth, 1967–
 Christmas and Hanukkah origami / by Ruth Owen.
     p. cm. — (Holiday origami)
 Includes index.
 ISBN 978-1-4488-7860-4 (library binding) — ISBN 978-1-4488-7919-9 (pbk.) — ISBN 978-1-4488-7925-0 (6-pack)
 1. Origami—Juvenile literature. 2. Christmas decorations—Juvenile literature.
 3. Hanukkah decorations—Juvenile literature. I. Title.
 TT870.O946 2013
 736'.982—dc23
                                                    2012009644

Manufactured in the United States of America

CPSIA Compliance Information: Batch # B4S12PK: For Further Information contact Rosen Publishing, New York, New York at 1-800-237-9932

Contents

Origami in Action

Origami is the art of folding paper to make small models, or **sculptures**.

Using just a single sheet of paper and some folding and creasing you can make a Star of David, a candle, a Christmas tree, or even Santa Claus!

No one knows when people first began making models from paper. One place where origami has been a popular art form for hundreds of years is Japan. The word "origami" comes from the Japanese words "ori" which means "folding," and "kami" which means "paper."

If you've never tried origami before, that's no problem. This book will take you step-by-step through some fun origami projects to make this Christmas and Hanukkah. All you need is some paper and to get folding and creasing!

4

Get Folding!

Before you get started on your Christmas or Hanukkah origami models, here are some tips.

Tip 1

Read all the instructions carefully and look at the pictures. Make sure you understand what's required before you begin a fold. Don't rush, but be patient. Work slowly and carefully.

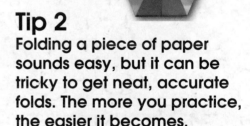

Tip 2

Folding a piece of paper sounds easy, but it can be tricky to get neat, accurate folds. The more you practice, the easier it becomes.

Tip 3

If an instruction says "crease," make the crease as flat as possible. The flatter the creases, the better the model. You can make a sharp crease by running a plastic ruler along the edge of the paper.

Tip 4

Sometimes, at first, your models may look a little crumpled. Don't give up! The more models you make, the better you will get at folding and creasing.

When it comes to origami, practice makes perfect!

Just take a look at this origami Christmas tree and basket of colorful stars made by an experienced model maker. Keep practicing and you could become an origami master!

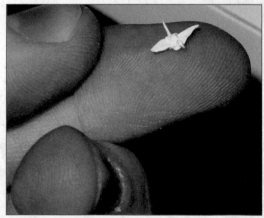

One of the most common origami models made in Japan is a type of bird called a crane. The crane below has been made using patterned paper. Origami model makers use single color and patterned paper. You can even use a page from a magazine, or a dollar bill!

Check out this miniature origami crane. Now that takes extreme origami skill!

Christmas Tree

All over the world, billions of people, including those who do not celebrate Jesus' birth, enjoy the festivities of Christmas.

One important **tradition** is the decorating of a Christmas tree. Evergreen trees were first cut down, brought indoors, and decorated in Germany in the 1500s. In the 1800s, Christmas trees became popular in the United States. Trees were decorated with handmade paper snowflakes and stars, paper baskets filled with sugared almonds, beads, small toys, and real burning candles!

To make a Christmas tree, you will need:

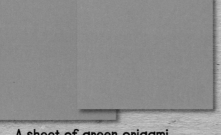

A sheet of green origami paper for each tree

Buttons and beads for decorations

Glue

(Origami paper is sometimes colored on both sides or white on one side.)

STEP 1:
Place the paper colored side down. Fold the paper diagonally, and crease.

STEP 2:
Fold both sides into the center along the dotted lines, and crease.

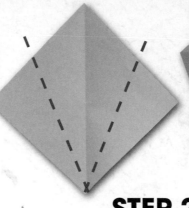

STEP 3:
Turn the model over. Fold in both sides along the dotted lines, and crease. The sides should meet at the model's center crease, as seen to the right.

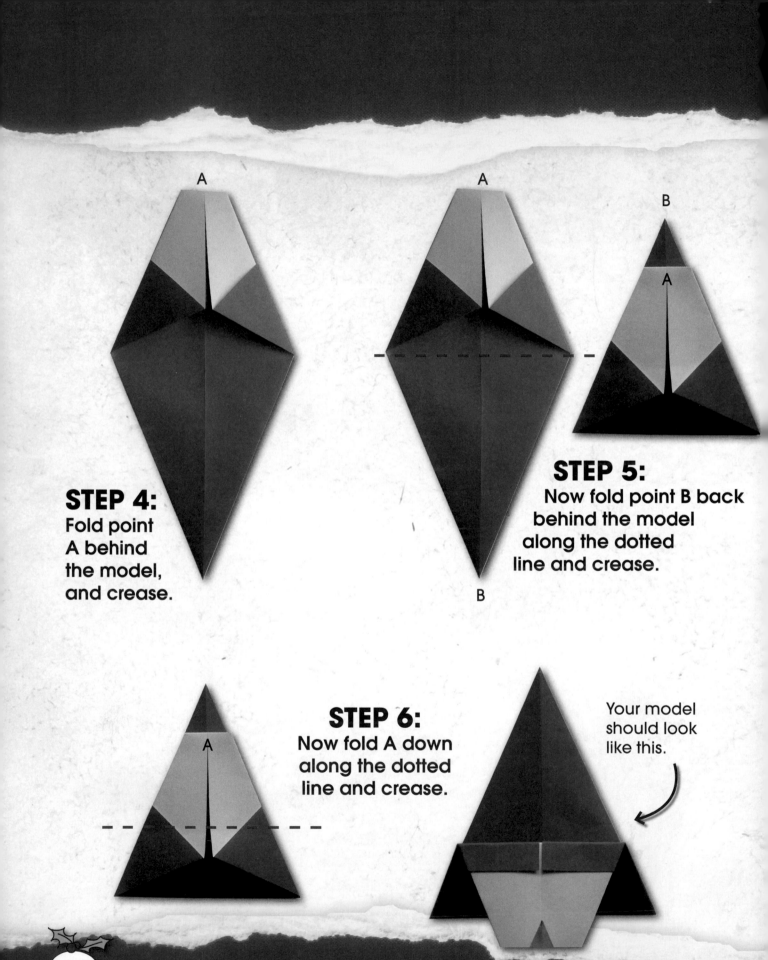

STEP 4:
Fold point A behind the model, and crease.

STEP 5:
Now fold point B back behind the model along the dotted line and crease.

STEP 6:
Now fold A down along the dotted line and crease.

Your model should look like this.

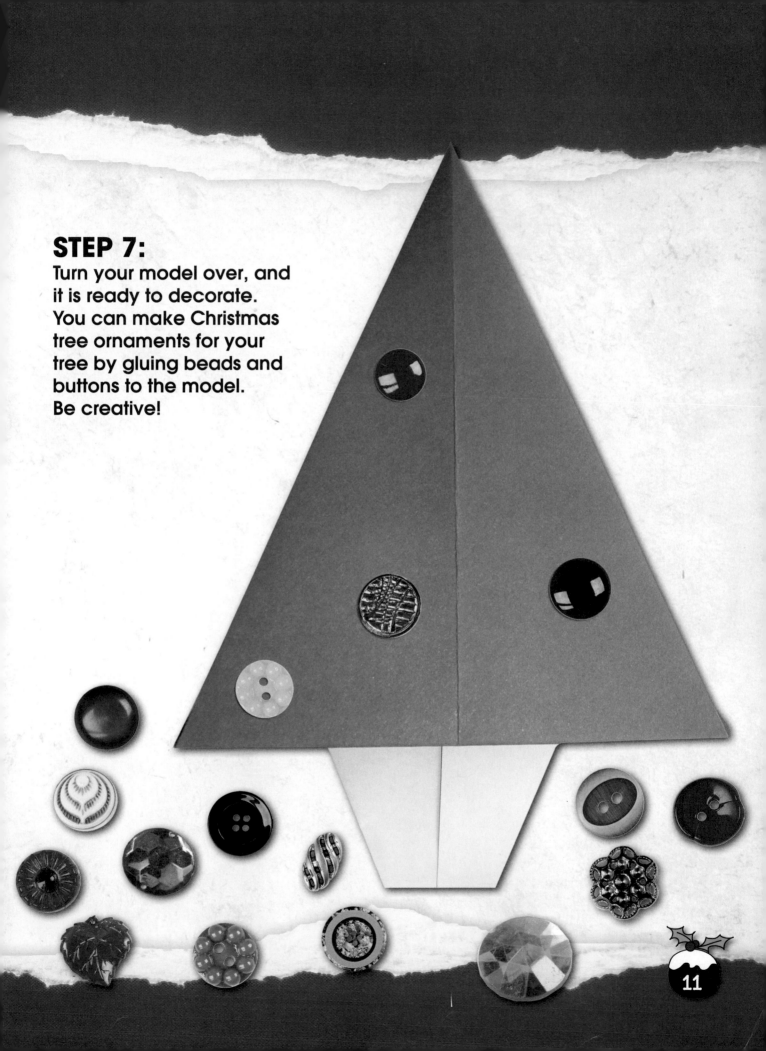

STEP 7:
Turn your model over, and it is ready to decorate. You can make Christmas tree ornaments for your tree by gluing beads and buttons to the model. Be creative!

Origami Santa Claus

Did you know that not everyone calls the man in the red suit Santa Claus? In Britain, he is called Father Christmas. In some countries, he is called St. Nicholas, probably after a kindly fourth-century Christian saint. In the Netherlands, St. Nicholas is "Sinterklaas," which is probably where the modern name "Santa Claus" comes from.

And did you know that Santa didn't always wear red? In the past, he was described as wearing green and other colored outfits. In the 1800s, he emerged as a jolly figure dressed in red. The look of Santa we all know and love today was actually made popular in ads for a famous cola drink in the 1930s!

To make an origami Santa, you will need:

A sheet of red
origami paper

Peel and stick
goggly eyes

(Origami paper is sometimes colored on both sides or white on one side.)

STEP 1:
Place the paper colored side down. Fold the paper diagonally, along both lines, and crease.

STEP 2:
Fold the top point down to meet the center, and crease.

STEP 3:
Fold the point back up again, and crease.

STEP 4:
Unfold the crease you've just made. Now fold the point up again to meet the crease from the last fold.

STEP 5:
Fold the flap up one more time, tucking the point underneath, and crease.

STEP 6:
Now fold up the bottom point so that it meets the top of the model.

STEP 7:
Now fold the bottom point back down again. You've just made Santa's beard!

STEP 8:
Turn the model over and fold in both sides along the dotted lines.

STEP 9:
Now fold both sides in along the dotted lines so that they meet in the model's center. Crease both sides well.

14

STEP 10:
Fold the right side of the model into the center, and crease.

STEP 11:
Now fold the right side back on itself, and crease well. This should form a square shape.

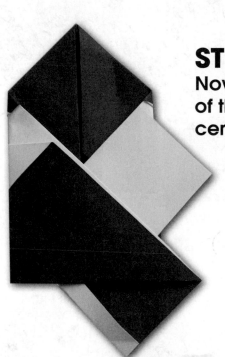

STEP 12:
Now fold the left side of the model into the center, and crease.

STEP 13:
Now fold the left side back on itself, to form a square shape. Crease well.

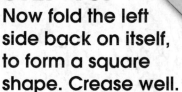

STEP 14:
Turn the model over and your Santa is complete. Stick on goggly eyes and give your Santa a nose or mouth.

Make a Christmas Card

The first commercially produced Christmas cards were probably sent in England in the 1840s. Early Christmas cards usually featured flowers, fairies, and other designs that reminded people of the coming of spring.

In the United States, the first printed cards were produced in the 1870s. Soon after this, postcards became a favorite way of sending Christmas greetings. By the 1920s, however, cards with envelopes once again became popular.

Today, Christians and non-Christians alike celebrate the holiday season, and the huge variety of cards available express many different sentiments, from "Merry Christmas" to "Happy Holidays" and "Seasons Greetings."

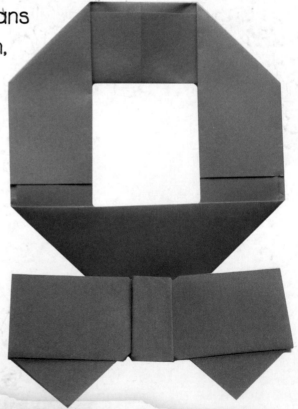

Now you can make your own Christmas cards featuring this origami wreath and bow.

To make a Christmas card, you will need:

Glue

One sheet of green origami paper and one sheet in your favorite color

A piece of construction paper 8 inches (20 cm) by 6 inches (15 cm)

Scissors

(Origami paper is sometimes colored on both sides or white on one side.)

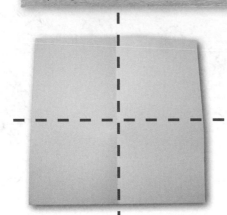

STEP 1:

To make the wreath, place the green sheet of paper colored side down. Fold the paper along both lines, and crease.

STEP 2:

Now cut the paper in half. Take one half and fold it into thirds along the dotted lines. Fold each side into the center, and crease.

STEP 3:

Now fold both sides into the center along the dotted lines, and crease.

STEP 4:

Repeat steps 2 and 3 with the other half of the paper. You should now have two halves of your wreath. Slide A into B and C into D, and push together.

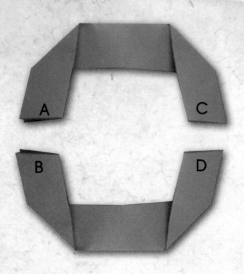

STEP 5:

Your wreath is complete and should look like this.

STEP 6:

To make the bow, repeat step 1. Then fold two sides into the center, and crease.

STEP 7:

Fold down the corners of the bottom flap, and crease.

STEP 8:

Now fold over the top half of the model, and crease.

Your model should look like this.

STEP 9:

Now make four folds along the dotted lines, and fold the model into the center. These folds are known as step folds.

STEP 10:

Close up the four folds you've just made. Your model should look like this.

STEP 11:

Now fold back the four corners at the center of the model, and crease well.

STEP 12:

Turn the model over and your bow is ready to be glued to the wreath. Fold a piece of construction paper in half and glue the wreath and bow to the card. Write a holiday greeting on the front.

Merry Christmas!

Origami Menorah

Hanukkah, also called the Festival of Lights, celebrates a **miracle** that happened to the Jewish people 2,000 years ago. At that time, the Jews were ruled by the Syrian-Greeks who tried to force them to abandon their religion. The Jews fought back and won. When the Jews tried to rededicate their temple by lighting a holy lamp, there was only enough oil for one day. The story of the miracle says that the oil lasted for eight days, however, until more oil arrived.

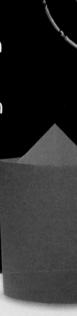

At Hanukkah, Jews light candles every evening in a candlestick known as the menorah. The menorah holds eight candles, for the eight days, and a ninth candle, which is used to light the others.

To make an origami menorah, you will need:

9 sheets each of orange and blue origami paper

Double-sided tape

(Origami paper is sometimes colored on both sides or white on one side.)

In this project you can make nine origami Hanukkah candles and create your own paper menorah.

STEP 1:

To make a blue candle with an orange flame, you will need to fold two sheets of paper at once.

Put the sheets of paper together, white sides touching. You can use a small piece of double-sided tape to hold them together if you wish.

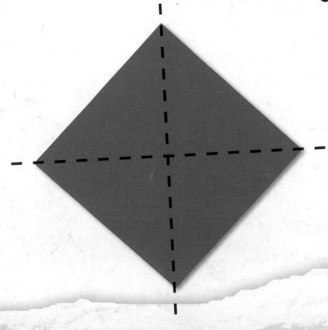

STEP 2:

Place the paper blue side down, fold along the dotted lines, and crease.

STEP 3:

Now fold two opposite points into the center so they touch the center crease, and crease both folds well. Remember, it's important that you make your creases very sharp for this model because you are working with two sheets of paper.

STEP 4:

Now fold down the top point, and crease well.

STEP 5:

Now fold up the bottom point along the dotted line. You can change where you make this fold to get a bigger or smaller flame. The higher the fold, the bigger the flame.

This point will be the flame

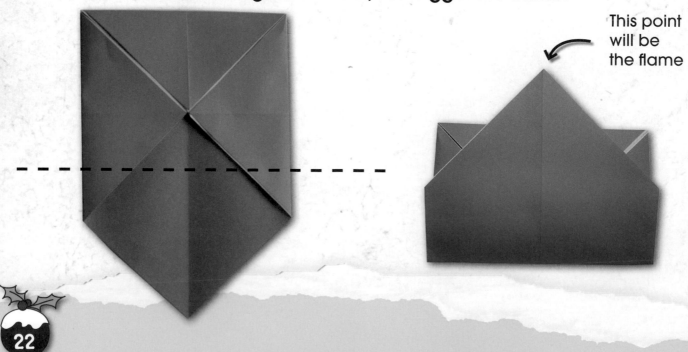

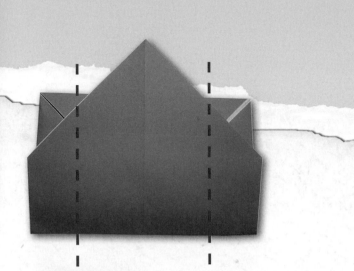

STEP 6:
Now fold in both sides along the dotted lines. The paper will be very thick, so you will need to crease the folds hard.

STEP 7:
The back of your model should now look like this. If you wish, you can use tape to hold the two folded sides in place.

STEP 8:
Turn the model over, and your Hanukkah candle is ready. Now make another eight candles and set up your origami menorah. You can place your candles in a line or in a group like this.

Raise up one candle to be the "shamash" or "helper candle," which is the candle used to light the others.

Origami Dreidel

At Hanukkah, children play a game with a four-sided spinning top called a dreidel. A dreidel has the **Hebrew** letters nun, gimel, hay, and shin on its sides.

To play the dreidel game, each player puts a piece of gelt (a candy coin) into a pile. Taking turns, the players spin the dreidel. If the nun is facing up when the dreidel stops, the player gets nothing. If gimel is showing, the player gets everything in the pile. Hay gives a player half the pile, and shin means the player has to put a coin in.

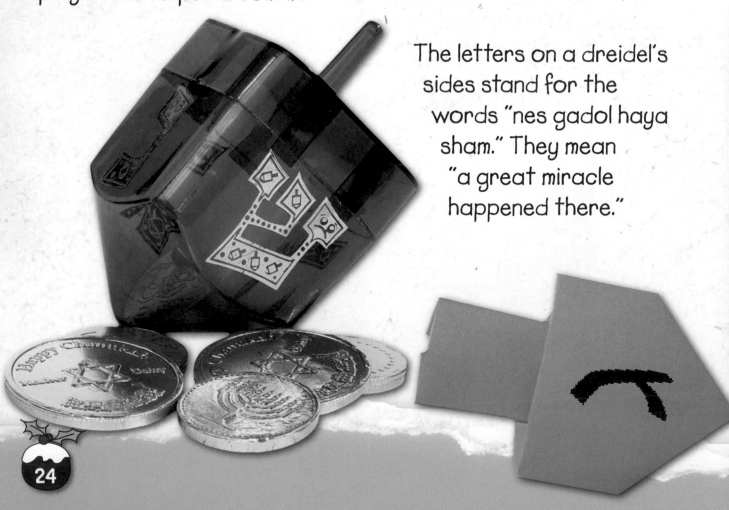

The letters on a dreidel's sides stand for the words "nes gadol haya sham." They mean "a great miracle happened there."

To make origami dreidels, you will need:

Sheets of origami paper in your favorite colors

Black marker

(Origami paper is sometimes colored on both sides or white on one side.)

STEP 1:
Place the paper colored side down. Fold the paper in half, and crease.

STEP 2:
Fold up the two bottom corners of the square so they meet in the center, and crease.

STEP 3:
Fold in the two sides so they meet in the center, and crease.

STEP 4:
Fold down the top of the model to meet the bottom point, and crease. Your model should look like this.

STEP 5:
Fold the bottom flap back up along the dotted line, and crease.

STEP 6:
Now fold up points A and B, and crease well.

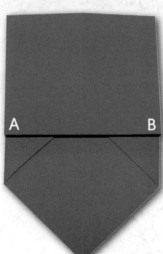

A   B

STEP 7:
Now unfold the two creases you've just made.

STEP 8:
Fold the right side of the model into the center. A small triangle will spread open at the crease you made in step 6. Repeat on the left side.

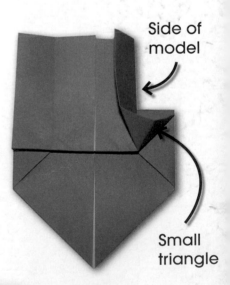

Side of model

Small triangle

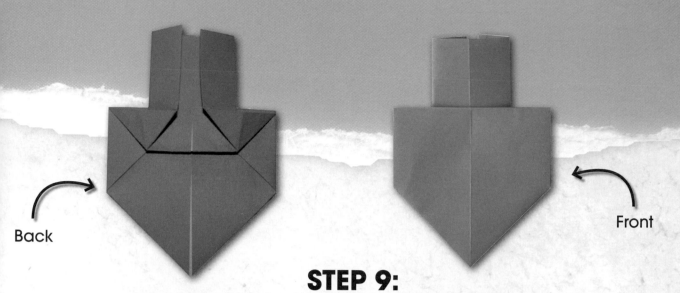

Back

Front

STEP 9:
Crease the sides well and flatten the triangles.
Turn the model over, and your dreidel is complete.

STEP 10:
Make dreidels in different colors and string them together to create
Hanukkah decorations. Draw on the Hebrew letters nun, gimel, hay,
and shin using a black marker.

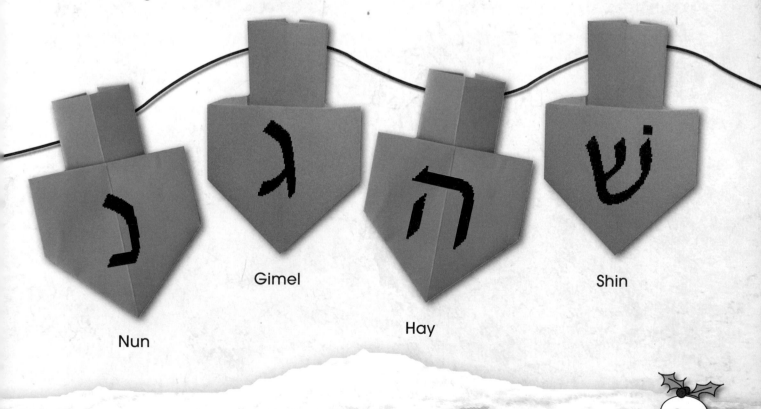

Nun

Gimel

Hay

Shin

Star of David

Hanukkah is a time for giving gifts and getting together with family. Decorate your home for the festivities with these origami Hanukkah stars.

The six-pointed "Jewish star," or Star of David, has been the recognized **symbol** of the Jewish people for centuries. It has been used as a symbol on Jewish religious objects, prayer books, and buildings for over a thousand years.

You can make your Hanukkah stars in shades of blue, or blue and white. Blue and white are the colors of the *tallit*, a prayer shawl worn by some Jews when they are praying. These colors have become associated with Jewish people and celebrations.

To make Hanukkah stars, you will need:

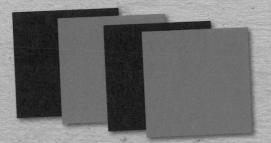

2 sheets of origami paper
for each star

Glue

(Origami paper is sometimes colored on both sides or white on one side.)

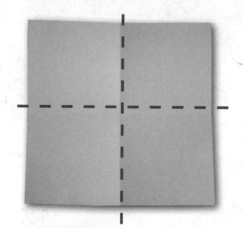

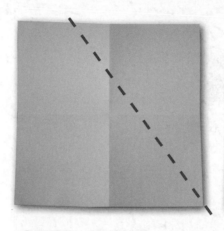

STEP 1:
Place a piece of paper colored side down. Make two folds along the dotted lines, and crease.

STEP 2:
Now fold the right side of the paper along the dotted line, and crease.

STEP 3:
Now fold the left side along the dotted line, and crease.

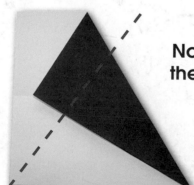

STEP 4:
Unfold the crease you've just made. Fold the top of the model along the dotted line, and crease.

STEP 5:
Your model should now look like this.

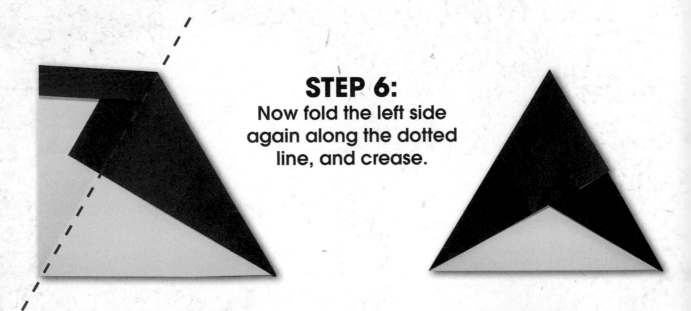

STEP 6:
Now fold the left side again along the dotted line, and crease.

STEP 7:
Turn the model over, and the first section of your star is complete.

STEP 8:

Now take another sheet of paper and repeat steps 1 to 7. When you have two triangle-shaped sections, glue them together to make a star.

STEP 9:

Make lots of stars and string them together to create Hanukkah decorations.

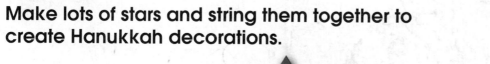

Glossary

Hebrew (HEE-broo) The language of the Jewish people and of others living in Israel. Hebrew is also the language in which most of the Old Testament, or Hebrew Bible, is written.

miracle (MEER-uh-kul) An unexpected and favorable event that is not easily explained by science and that some may consider to be the work of God or some other supreme being.

origami (or-uh-GAH-mee) The art of folding paper into decorative shapes or objects.

sculptures (SKULP-cherz) Works of art that have a shape to them, such as statues or carved objects, and may be made of wood, stone, metal, plaster, or even paper.

symbol (SIM-bul) Something that stands for or represents another thing, such as an important event or person. A cross may be a symbol of Christianity.

tradition (truh-DIH-shun) A custom, belief, or practice that has existed for a long time and has been passed on from one generation to the next.

Index

Websites

Due to the changing nature of Internet links, PowerKids Press has developed an online list of websites related to the subject of this book. This site is updated regularly. Please use this link to access the list:
www.powerkidslinks.com/horig/cah/